The Science of Birds

LIVING SCIENCE

Janice Parker

Gareth Stevens Publishing
MILWAUKEE

For a free color catalog describing Gareth Stevens' list of high-quality books and multimedia programs, call 1-800-542-2595 (USA) or 1-800-461-9120 (Canada). Gareth Stevens Publishing's Fax: (414) 225-0377.

Library of Congress Cataloging-in-Publication Data

Parker, Janice.
   The science of birds / by Janice Parker.
      p. cm. — (Living science)
   Includes index.
   Summary: Provides information about the life cycles, physical characteristics, habitats, behavior, and ecological importance of birds.
   ISBN 0-8368-2465-2 (lib. bdg.)
   1. Birds — Juvenile literature. [1. Birds] I. Title. II. Series: Living science (Milwaukee, Wis.)
QL676.2.P364 1999
598 — dc21   99-28912

This edition first published in 1999 by
Gareth Stevens Publishing
1555 North RiverCenter Drive, Suite 201
Milwaukee, WI 53212 USA

Project Co-ordinator: Samantha McCrory
Series Editor: Leslie Strudwick
Copy Editor: Rennay Craats
Design and Illustration: Warren Clark
Cover Design: Carole Knox
Layout: Lucinda Cage
Gareth Stevens Editor: Patricia Lantier-Sampon

Every reasonable effort has been made to trace ownership and to obtain permission to reprint copyright material. The publishers would be pleased to have any errors or omissions brought to their attention so that they may be corrected in subsequent printings.

Photograph Credits:
Corel Corporation: cover (center), pages 4, 5, 7, 8 top left, 8 top right, 8 bottom left, 9, 10, 11, 14, 16, 17, 18 right, 19, 20, 21 bottom, 22, 23 top, 23 bottom left, 24, 25, 27, 28, 29 top, 30; Ivy Images: page 15 top (Fred Bird/Spectrum Stock); PhotoDisc: cover (background); Robert S. Schemenauer: page 15 bottom; Tom Stack & Associates: pages 6 bottom left (Dominique Braud), 6 top left (Dominique Braud), 6 bottom right (John Gerlach), 13 bottom (Tom Stack), 23 center (Jeff Foott), 29 bottom (David M. Dennis), 31 (David M. Dennis); J.D. Taylor: pages 23 bottom right, 26; Visuals Unlimited: pages 6 top right (Rob Simpson), 8 bottom right (John D. Cunningham), 12 (Patricia Armstrong), 13 top (Jeff Greenberg), 13 far right (Arthur Morris), 18 left (Patrick J. Endres), 21 top (Rick Poley), 21 far right (D. Cavagnaro).

Printed in Canada

1 2 3 4 5 6 7 8 9 03 02 01 00 99

Contents

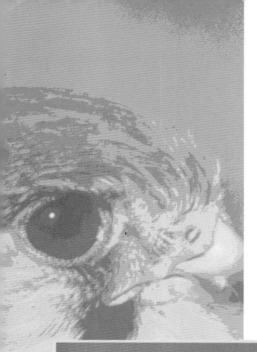

What Do You Know about Birds?

Birds are a type of animal. Mammals, reptiles, **amphibians**, fish, and insects are other types of animals. Birds are also vertebrates. This means they have a backbone. Many different **species** of birds live in the world. All birds share similar features and habits.

The hummingbird was given its name because of the humming sound its wings make.

Most birds fly, but some birds cannot. All birds lay eggs. Also, they all have bills. Other animals share some of these features with birds.

However, all birds have one feature that no other animal has — feathers. Other animals may be covered in fur, hair, or scales, but never in feathers. Whether or not a bird can fly, it has feathers covering its body.

Macaws are large parrots. They have brightly colored feathers and long, pointed tails.

Puzzler

Name all the birds you can think of that cannot fly. How many can you identify?

Answer: Here is a list of some flightless birds: cassowaries, emus, kiwis, ostriches, and penguins.

Life Cycles

All plants and animals have a life cycle. They all begin life, grow, reproduce, and die. Like all other living things, birds have a life cycle.

A bird begins its life inside an egg. When the egg hatches, a tiny bird comes out. It grows into an adult bird and leaves its parents' nest. One day this bird will lay eggs of its own.

Some birds are blind and without feathers when they hatch out of their eggs. They must rely on their parents for food and protection. Other birds are able to live on their own soon after hatching.

When young birds are strong enough, they leave their parents to start their own lives. They will mate and have baby birds of their own.

Puzzler

Why are some types of birds ready to leave the nest earlier than others?

Answer: When a baby bird decides to leave the nest depends on its parents. Some types of bird parents give very little care to the young birds once they have hatched. These baby birds must be able to feed themselves quickly. Other types of bird parents stay with their young for weeks or months.

Feet and Bills

To keep track of the many different types of birds, scientists group them by their features. Feet and bills are an easy way to tell the difference between birds. The feet and bills can tell us what a bird eats and in what type of area it lives.

Types of Feet

A goose's large, webbed feet work like paddles in the water.

A sparrow uses its perching feet to stand on branches.

An owl's strong feet help it grasp its **prey**.

An ostrich's feet are designed for running and carrying its heavy body.

Activity

Looking at Birds

Search through magazines and books for photographs of birds. Look at the birds' bills and feet. Try to decide what types of food the birds might eat, or where they might live.

Types of Bills

A flamingo's bill picks up the tiny plants that it eats from the water.

A pelican's bill allows it to scoop up fish.

A hummingbird's bill is long. The bird can put its bill deep into large flowers to collect nectar.

A pigeon's bill makes it easy for the bird to pick up small seeds and fruit.

An eagle's bill works like a knife to tear its prey.

A parrot's strong bill can crack nuts and fruits.

Types of Birds

Nearly nine thousand species of birds exist in the world. Scientists put every bird in one of twenty-seven groups, or orders. Birds in the same order have similar features. Here are some of the bird orders and their features:

Types

Birds of Prey	Perching Birds	Hummingbirds and Swifts	Owls
• eat other animals • excellent fliers	• biggest group of birds • feet are designed for grasping branches • live over land	• often live in tropical habitats • strong, fast fliers • very small	• eat other animals • more than 140 different types • usually hunt at night

Examples

eagle, falcon, osprey	blue jay, chickadee, swallow	chimney swift, ruby-throated hummingbird	hawk owl, screech owl, snowy owl

Puzzler

To which group does the crow belong?

Answer:
Crows belong in the perching group. They live over land and are related to blue jays.

Penguins	Pigeons and Doves	Waterfowl	Ostrich
• 17 different types • live in warm and cold habitats • swim well	• feathers are stiff and smooth • have a plump body • live all over the world	• build nests near bodies of water • dive underwater to find food • webbed feet	• flightless • largest bird • only bird in its group

chinstrap, emperor, Galápagos

crowned pigeon, inca dove, mourning dove

mute swan, snow goose, wood duck

ostrich

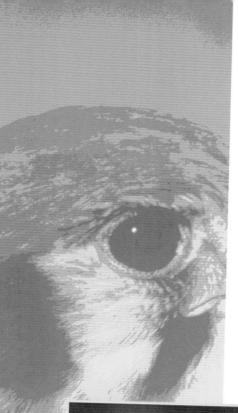

Working with Birds

If you love birds, you may want to get a job where you can work with them. Many types of careers involve birds. Zookeepers, biologists, and **poultry** farmers all may work with birds. Ornithology is the study of birds. Ornithologists work to learn more about birds. They also try to help save **endangered** birds. In order to become an ornithologist, you have to study the science of animals at a university. Even if you do not work with birds, you can still be a birdwatcher. There are many birdwatching clubs around the world.

If scientists want to keep track of a bird, they carefully place a small, metal identification tag around the bird's leg.

Many zoos have a bird sanctuary, where parrots and other birds are given large, open spaces for flying.

Birdwatching

Go outdoors and see how many different types of birds you can spot. If possible, bring binoculars and a book with pictures and names of birds that live in your area. Bring a pencil and paper to write down what you see. Note where and when you saw a bird.

Turkeys are raised on poultry farms.

Birds and People

Birds are important to humans for many different reasons. People sometimes keep birds, such as canaries, as pets. Many birds are quite happy to live with people.

Some people love to watch birds in the wild. These birdwatchers will often go out into the wilderness early in the morning, hoping to see certain birds. Birdwatchers often make lists of the different birds they have seen. Over time, some birdwatchers might see hundreds of different types of birds.

Parrots are great pets. They can learn to **mimic** sounds and words.

Bird feathers can be used in clothing and other items. Many homes have pillows or comforters that are filled with feathers and down. Down is especially good at keeping people warm. The warmest jackets and sleeping bags often contain down.

People eat certain kinds of birds, such as turkey, chicken, duck, or goose. Most people also eat chickens' eggs.

Activity

Looking at Eggs

Crack a chicken's egg into a dish. Look closely at the shell. An eggshell protects growing birds from the outside world. Eggshells are quite strong. The yellow part of the egg is called the **yolk**. If a young bird lived in the egg, it would eat the yolk as it grew. The clear part of the egg is called the egg white, or **albumen**. The albumen protects the growing bird. It also provides the bird with liquid and vitamins.

The Ukrainian culture values Easter eggs as symbols of spring and new life. This giant **pysanka** is in a town in Alberta, Canada. The egg is decorated with traditional Ukrainian designs.

Our Feathered Friends

irds have different kinds and colors of feathers. A small bird, such as a hummingbird, may have only 1,000 feathers. A large bird, such as a swan, may have over 25,000. Most birds have four different types of feathers. Down feathers are the soft ones close to the bird's body. These feathers help keep the bird warm. Most of the bird is covered with body feathers. Tail feathers help the bird keep its balance. Tail feathers are also often used to help attract mates. Wing feathers help a bird fly or move around.

wing feathers

body feathers

tail feathers

Baby birds are usually covered in down feathers.

Most feathers have four parts. The shaft is the stiff, stick-like section in the middle of the feather. Vanes are attached to the shaft. Barbs are attached to the vanes. Tiny barbules come out from the barbs.

Birds spend a lot of time **preening** their feathers. Combing through feathers with their beaks helps keep the feathers oiled and working well.

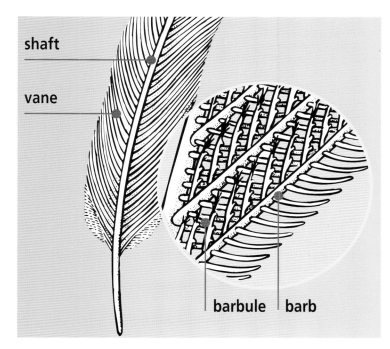

Activity

A Close Look at Feathers

Try to find a feather from any type of bird. Place the feather on a light-colored piece of paper. Look closely at the feather. Can you see the barbs? Is the feather flat and shiny or soft and fluffy? Try to guess which type of bird the feather came from.

Habitat

Birds live all over the world. They live in tropical forests and in hot deserts. Some live at sea. Some even live in the cold polar regions. Birds can live in such various habitats because they have adapted to them. Different types of birds have developed special features that help them live in different environments.

Arctic birds
have adapted to living in cold, snowy areas.
The snowy owl's white feathers help it hide from its prey. The feet of snowy owls are covered by soft, warm feathers that look like fur.

Cliff dwellers
have adapted to living and laying eggs on the edges of steep cliffs.
The murre does not make a nest. It lays its eggs on a ledge. The eggs are pointy at one end. If a murre egg is knocked around, it will roll in circles, like a top. The egg will not roll off the ledge.

Wading birds

have adapted to living near lakes, streams, and marshes.
The crowned crane has very long legs. This lets the bird wander through water in search of food.

Water birds

have adapted to swimming and taking off from water.
Swans have large, webbed feet. These feet are shaped like paddles and help the swan swim. A swan's long neck allows it to dip its head underwater to search for food.

City birds

have adapted to living near people.
Pigeons and crows will eat almost anything. They are not shy around people.

Puzzler

In what ways is the penguin adapted to swimming?

Answer:
The penguin's body shape helps it move easily through water. Penguin wings work like rudders to help the bird change direction while swimming. The feet are webbed and work like paddles. The penguin's body is covered in shiny, waterproof feathers that dry quickly.

Avoiding Danger

Most birds have ways to avoid becoming another animal's dinner. **Camouflage** helps many birds avoid being caught and eaten. Often, a bird can be heard in a tree, but cannot be seen. In many bird species, the female bird is a dull, spotted color while the male is more colorful. This keeps the female well-hidden when she sits on her nest.

Can you tell which mallard duck is female, and which is male?

Many birds' eggs are also camouflaged. Terns lay their eggs on the ground in a nest made of stones. The eggs are spotted and dull in color. They look just like the surrounding stones. The large eggs of an emu are a dark green color. The emu lays its eggs in dark green grasses.

Many birds simply fly away to avoid danger. Only a fast animal can catch a bird if it takes flight. Owls eat other birds. They can catch other birds by surprising them. Owls quickly and quietly swoop down and grab their prey.

Puzzler

A robin's eggs are a light blue color that is easy to see in the nest. Why do you think they are so colorful?

Answer: The adult robin stays on its nest covering the eggs. The eggs are almost always hidden by the parent. If the robin does leave the nest, the egg color might help it find the nest again quickly.

Building a Nest

Most birds build nests. Nests are like cradles for the eggs and young birds. Nests come in many shapes and sizes. Hummingbirds are the smallest birds in the world. A hummingbird nest has only enough room for two tiny eggs and one parent. Eagle nests are very large. One eagle nest can weigh up to one ton.

Nests can be made from different materials. Anything a bird can carry might end up in a nest. Feathers, fur, grass, and moss all help to make nests. Some nests are made from mud. Birds will even add bits of garbage, such as tin foil or string, to their nests.

Birds build nests in water, on the ground, in trees, and on cliffs.

Ovenbirds make their nests out of clay and mud. It takes thousands of trips for the birds to carry the mud to the nest. The nests look like small clay ovens.

Activity

Spot a Bird's Nest

Next time you go outdoors, look up into trees to see if you can spot a nest. If you see bits of dried grass or twigs in a tree, it could be a nest. Larger nests, such as those made by crows, are usually easy to see.

Some birds let other birds do their work. Cowbirds lay their eggs in the nest of another type of bird. The other bird will care for the eggs and even feed the young birds after they hatch.

Woodpeckers make a nest inside hollow areas in tree trunks.

Weaver birds live in Africa. The male birds use their beaks to weave round nests in trees. They sit in the nest's entrance and flap their wings to attract female birds.

Web of Life

All living things depend on other living things to survive. Every plant and animal has its place in nature. If humans do not interfere with nature, the environment stays in balance. A food chain shows how animals survive by eating plants or other animals. Energy is transferred from one living thing to another in a food chain. When many food chains are connected, it is called a food web.

Birds play a very important role in a food web. They eat insects that we consider pests. Some birds also eat small mammals that disturb farmers.

Food Web

bald eagle

black-tailed prairie dog

grasshopper

grass and plants

A food web can begin with a plant. Insects, such as grasshoppers, eat the leaves of many different plants. Prairie dogs eat grasses and occasionally grasshoppers. Prairie dogs are food for bald eagles.

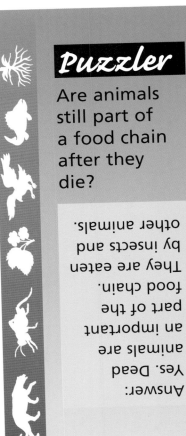

Puzzler

Are animals still part of a food chain after they die?

Answer: Yes. Dead animals are an important part of the food chain. They are eaten by insects and other animals.

Protecting Birds

Hopefully, birds will always be a part of our world. However, many bird species are endangered. People are often the main reason birds are in trouble, since they have killed many types of birds. The dodo bird once lived on islands in the Indian Ocean. Sailors killed and ate many dodos. Dodos became **extinct** more than three hundred years ago.

The passenger pigeon is also extinct. At one time, millions of passenger pigeons flew in the skies. People took over forest land to build homes and towns. The pigeons had nowhere to live. Humans also hunted the wild pigeons extensively. The last passenger pigeon died in captivity in the Cincinnati Zoo in 1914.

Today, passenger pigeons can only be seen in natural history museums.

Bald eagles are threatened because of the large numbers killed by hunters and trappers. Pollution and the rapid growth of farms and cities have contributed to the loss of their habitat.

Today, most people are trying to save endangered birds. For example, pollution nearly destroyed peregrine falcons. Scientists worked to help **captive** peregrines lay eggs. The new birds were then released into the wild.

Puzzler

Chopping down trees in a forest can endanger birds. Why?

Answer: Birds build nests in the trees in a forest. They eat plants and insects that live in the forest. Without trees, the birds lose their homes.

27

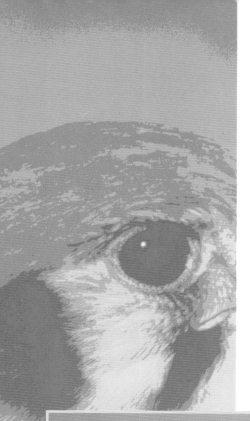

Singing Is for the Birds

We often hear birds singing even if we cannot see them. Bird sounds can be beautiful and distinctive. Many birds talk to one another through songs or calls. Birds have different sounding calls that mean different things. A bird may sing in order to attract a mate. It may send a message that it is in the area. Birds that live in **flocks** often make calls to warn other birds of danger.

Flocks of red-winged blackbirds sing their song repeatedly.

Birdwatchers listen to bird songs. Bird calls can help them locate a bird. Birdwatchers can tell what type of birds are in the area by their sounds. A scientist or birdwatcher may play a tape recording of certain bird sounds in order to attract birds.

The chickadee sounds like it is saying its own name when it sings. Its song sounds like *chick-a-dee-dee-dee*.

Scientists use special equipment to record bird songs.

The First Bird

Scientists believe birds **evolved** from reptiles. Feathers may have originally been scales. Flying reptiles called pterosaurs lived alongside the dinosaurs. Flying reptiles did not have feathers. Their wings were covered by skin, similar to bats' wings. Pterosaurs died out with the dinosaurs. Birds are not related to these animals. The first bird we know about lived more than 130 million years ago. **Fossils** of this animal, called Archaeopteryx, show that it was the first animal to have feathers. Archaeopteryx was about the size of a crow. Like reptiles, it had teeth and a tail.

Crocodiles and alligators are the closest living relatives to birds.

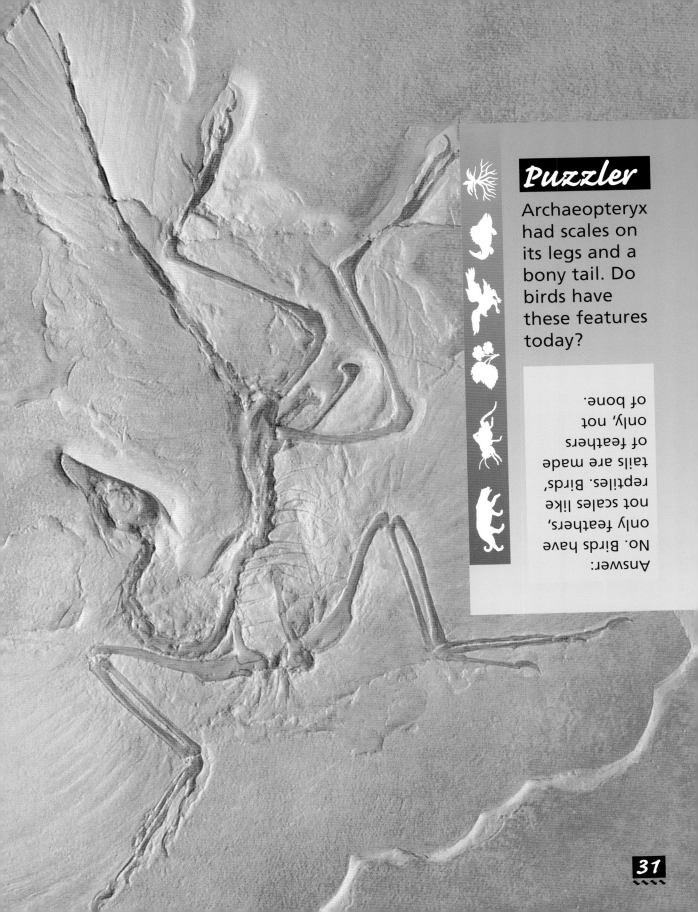

Puzzler

Archaeopteryx had scales on its legs and a bony tail. Do birds have these features today?

Answer: No. Birds have only feathers, not scales like reptiles. Birds' tails are made of feathers only, not of bone.

Glossary

albumen: the clear or white inside part of an egg.

amphibians: animals that live in water and on land.

camouflage: to blend in with the colors of the environment in order to stay hidden from predators.

captive: taken and held away from natural habitat; confined.

endangered: at risk of dying out completely.

evolve: to change shape or develop gradually over a long period of time.

extinct: no longer in existence.

flock: a group of birds.

fossils: the remains of plants or animals found hardened in layers of rock.

mimic: to copy speech, appearance, or actions.

poultry: birds, such as chickens and turkeys, kept for meat and eggs.

predators: animals that search out and eat other animals.

preening: when a bird uses its beak as a comb to keep its feathers clean and healthy.

prey: animals that are eaten by other animals.

pysanka: an Easter egg decorated with Ukrainian designs.

species: a group of closely-related animals or plants that are often similar in behavior and appearance.

yolk: the yellow inside part of an egg.

Index

Web Sites

www.enchantedlearning.com/subjects/birds

www.portalproductions.com/h/index.html

netvet.wustl.edu/e-zoo.htm

parrotjungle.com

Some web sites stay current longer than others. For further web sites, use your search engines to locate the following topics: *birdwatching*, *hummingbird*, *parrot*, and *pets*.